PLAY
FOOTBALL

PLAY
FOOTBALL

Coach and Technical Adviser Mark Drabwell
Written by Catherine Saunders
Photography by Russell Sadur

Contents

Introduction

You probably already know the basics of football — it is a game played between two teams of eleven players and the object is to score more goals than the other team. Sounds simple! But do you really know how to play the game like a pro? Do you know a driven pass from a swerve shot or a Cruyff turn from a drag back? Well, it's time to get your boots on and find out!

The Coach

All the techniques and skills in this book are carried out under the supervision of FA-qualified coach, Mark Drabwell. Mark holds a UEFA A Licence Diploma and is a Staff Coach for the English FA. He is committed to teaching the correct techniques and skills from an early age and regularly coaches children of all ages and abilities.

To get the most out of this book, read each page carefully. Make sure that you check out the step-by-step skills and helpful tips. Then get out there and start practising! The more you practise, the better you will become.

As you will see when you turn the page, kit has changed quite a bit since 1881!

HISTORY

Although a version of football can be traced back as far as the ancient Chinese, Greek and Roman civilisations, the modern game originated nearly 150 years ago in England. In 1863 association football and rugby football officially became two separate games and since that time football as we know it has spread all over the world. Today football's governing body, FIFA (Fédération Internationale de Football Association) has 207 member countries.

These players are ready to learn how to play football like their heroes!

Football shirts should be loose enough to give you freedom of movement.

Goalkeeping shirts are usually long-sleeved to keep goalkeepers warm.

Goalkeepers sometimes wear jogging bottoms in the winter.

Socks should be pulled up to keep your shin pads in place.

Football Kit

If you want to learn how to play like a professional footballer, you should start by getting the right kind of kit. Choosing kit is not about fashion. It is about safety, comfort and flexibility. Your kit should fit properly, especially your boots, so that you can move around the pitch as freely as possible.

Shin pads

Shins are easily injured so players protect them by wearing shin pads, even in training. Shin pads are worn under football socks and also protect the ankle.

Boots

Boots are the most important part of your kit. Football boots need to be flexible to allow all parts of your foot to move in any direction. They should also provide support and protection. To make sure you find the perfect fit, wear your football socks when you try on new boots. Balance is an important part of footballing technique so football boots have studs fixed to the sole to prevent players from slipping.

Astro boots

For training and matches on artificial surfaces, players wear astro boots. Astro boots have lots of small pimples on the sole but do not have enough grip to wear on grass, except in dry conditions.

Goalkeepers' kit

Goalkeepers wear a slightly different kit to outfield players. They need more protection, especially when making diving saves. Goalkeeping shirts are usually long-sleeved and padded at the shoulders and elbows while goalkeepers' shorts have extra padding to protect their hips.

Gloves

Goalkeepers wear gloves to protect their hands and give them extra grip on the ball. Gloves are made of strong but flexible materials such as latex so that goalkeepers can move their hands freely.

This is the view from the corner flag at Manchester United's home ground, Old Trafford.

The goal

One part of the pitch must always be the same size — the goal. Many years ago the size was set as eight feet high and eight yards wide which today translates as 2.44 metres high and 7.32 metres wide.

The Pitch

Mini pitches

Young players should not play on full-sized pitches. Instead they should concentrate on developing their techniques and match skills on special mini pitches with smaller goals.

You can play football anywhere — in your back garden, in the park or in the school playground — but the best place for a safe and skilful match is in on a proper pitch. There are lots of different types of pitch from natural surfaces such as grass to artificial surfaces which are great for indoor pitches.

The long and short of it

Not all football pitches are the same size. According to FIFA, the length of a pitch must be between 90 metres (100 yards) and 120 metres (130 yards) and the width not less than 45 metres (50 yards) and not more than 90 metres (100 yards). Of course, the length must always be greater than the width, otherwise the pitch would be square! Here are the key parts of the pitch:

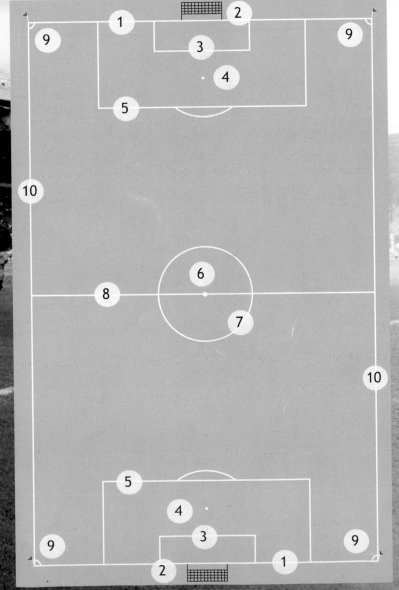

1 Goal line	6 Centre spot
2 Goal	7 Centre circle
3 6 yard box	8 Halfway line
4 Penalty spot	9 Corner arc
5 18 yard box	10 Touchline

Balls

Footballs also come in different sizes. Young players should use smaller balls to help improve their technique.

Shall we dance?

This fun warm-up helps to develop balance, ball control and co-ordination. The players are travelling forwards and placing alternate feet on top of the ball. Next the players have to do this while travelling backwards!

Try to look where you are going, rather than at the ball.

Quickly bring the right foot down and put the left foot on the ball.

Warm Up

It is important for teenagers and adults to warm up and stretch their muscles before exercising. However, young players' bodies are more supple and flexible so they only need a general warm up. The coach has developed fun ways of warming up the young players so that they are physically and mentally prepared for the game.

Throw, head, catch

It is reds versus blues and the object of the game is for one player to throw the ball, the next player to head it and the third to catch it. It might sound easy but this exercise requires teamwork, awareness and determination.

STAR PROS

Australia's national team is nicknamed the Socceroos. Before an important World Cup qualifying tie they start the warm up with some gentle jogging before moving onto individual muscle stretches and specialised ball work.

Through the gate

A team must get the ball between two cones to score a point. This game helps the players get used to running with the ball and passing. To be successful they must work together.

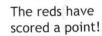

The reds have scored a point!

Fast hands

The players throw five footballs around in a circle, without dropping them. This tests co-ordination and communication. To make it even harder, the coach is timing them!

Passing

Players pass the ball so that their team keeps possession and moves towards the opposition's goal. A side foot pass (push pass) is perfect for short distances but has little power. A driven pass, using the laces (instep), is better for long distances.

Side foot pass

1 Place your non-kicking foot close to the side of the ball. Use your arms for balance and keep your eyes on the ball.

2 Swing your kicking leg back a short distance and strike the centre of the ball with the side of your foot. Use your arms for balance.

3 Follow through with your kicking leg to generate power. With this type of pass, the ball should stay on the ground.

Chip pass

A chip is a short pass that aims to go over your opponent's head and drop into the path of your team mate. Place your non-kicking foot next to the ball and strike the bottom of the ball upwards with a short, stabbing action.

Point your toes downwards and strike the base of the ball, with no follow through.

Driven pass

Place your non-kicking foot next to the ball. Swing your kicking leg back and bend it slightly so that your knee is over the ball. Point your toes downwards and strike the centre of the ball with your laces. Follow through with your kicking leg.

This pass is a great way to move the ball beyond an opponent or over a long distance.

Lean back slightly if you want to give the pass some height.

Use your arms to help you balance.

The approach is the same as for a side foot pass.

Striking the ball with your laces generates more power.

Long lofted kick

1 To kick the ball high and over a longer distance, stand behind the ball and take a run up. As you approach the ball, plant your non-kicking foot a little way from the ball and swing your kicking leg back.

2 Strike the bottom of the ball with your laces and follow through with your kicking foot.

Leaning back will help lift the ball and make it travel further.

Try to plant your non-kicking foot a little way from the ball.

Point your toes downwards as you prepare to strike the ball.

Kicking

By striking the ball with different parts of your foot, you can make it go almost anywhere you want. Good kicking technique will help you master more advanced skills so start with these two basic kicking techniques.

Inside foot

Place your non-kicking foot next to the ball. Turn your kicking foot outwards and strike the centre of the ball with the inside of your foot.

Outside foot

Stand at an angle with your feet apart and your non-kicking foot behind. Strike the centre of the ball with the outside of your foot.

Bending the ball

To make the ball bend you need to kick it off-centre on the opposite side to the direction you want it to go. So, if you want to swerve the ball to the left, strike it on the right and if you want to bend the ball to the right, strike it on the left. Using the inside of your foot bends the ball inwards and using the outside of your foot bends the ball outwards.

STAR PRO

England's **David Beckham** is perfectly poised to provide control, direction and power to a right-wing cross. He is also famous for his ability to bend free kicks around the wall and into the top corner of the goal.

Ball Control

Being able to get the ball under control with your first touch will really help your all-round game. The approach is the same, whether you control the ball with your head, chest, thigh or foot — keep your eyes on the ball and move your body in line with the flight of the ball. With practice you can learn to receive the ball at any height.

Chest control

Extend your arms, for balance and to keep them away from the ball. Keep your body relaxed and arch your back slightly. As the ball hits your chest, move your shoulders forwards so that the ball drops gently downwards.

TOP TIP

Relax your body when you are preparing to control the ball. If your body is stiff and tense you are more likely to mis-control it.

Side foot

Turn your foot to the side and, as it comes into contact with the ball, gently withdraw it to take the pace off the ball. Now try the same thing with the outside of your foot!

Laces

Great players can use their laces to control the ball. Bring your laces up to meet the ball and at the moment of impact bring your foot (and the ball) to the ground.

The wedge

As the ball comes towards you, lift your foot up and trap it between the sole of your foot and the ground. This technique brings the ball to a complete stop.

Thigh

Lean back slightly and use your arms for balance. Bend your standing leg a little and get your thigh in line with the ball. As the ball drops towards you, relax your thigh so that it forms a soft cushion and the ball drops downwards.

Don't lean back too much — it might make you lose your balance!

Use your thigh when the ball is too high to control with your foot or too low to control with your chest.

STAR PRO

With practice, any player can master ball control. Here, Spanish striker **Fernando Morientes** has remarkably light control for a player of his height and strength.

Heading

During a match the ball is not always played to your feet so you will often need to use your head to pass, control, clear or score. Heading is a key technique and it is important that you learn how to do it safely and effectively.

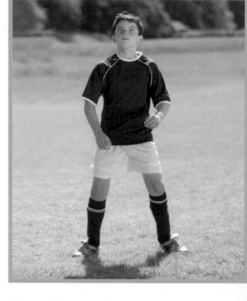

TOP TIP

Head the ball with the middle of your forehead. Never use the top or side of your head as it will be painful, dangerous and also less accurate.

Heading stance

There are three types of header but they all start from the same basic position. As the ball comes towards you, plant your feet firmly on the ground. Keep your eyes on the ball and relax your body.

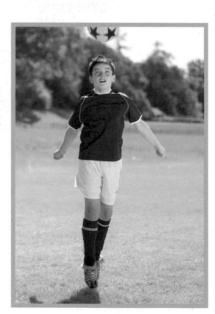

Basic header

Lean back a little so that your head and body are slightly behind the ball. Use your feet to push off and strike the ball with your forehead.

Defensive header

Push off from one foot and, as you jump, strike the bottom of the ball with your forehead. The ball should travel as far and as high as possible.

Attacking header

Strike the top or centre of the ball with your forehead and aim it downwards. This might create a goalscoring chance for yourself or a team mate!

Remember to strike the ball with your forehead.

Keep your eyes on the ball.

Bend your knees for extra power.

STAR PRO

Italy's captain **Paolo Maldini** is his country's record international. He is comfortable playing anywhere in defence. Here he soars commandingly above **Joahan Rodriguez** of Mexico to head the ball.

Dribbling practice

The best way to improve your dribbling skills is to practise. Line up some cones about two metres apart and dribble around them. The more you do it, the more skilful you will become. Soon you will be a confident dribbler!

Look up after every two or three touches.

Use the inside and outside of both feet!

See how fast you can go without losing control of the ball.

Dribbling

Dribbling is a way of moving the ball upfield. The player runs with the ball close to his or her feet and pushes it forwards with lots of small, quick kicks. Dribbling is all about close control — without this a player will lose possession easily. The best dribblers are able to control the ball even in crowded goal areas.

Balance is an important part of dribbling. Good balance will allow you to change direction quickly, without losing control. You should use plenty of small kicks with the inside and outside of both feet plus the laces and try to look up, rather than at your feet.

Dribbling technique

1 Keep your body relaxed and try to look where you are going every so often, rather than just at your feet. Push the ball forwards a short way using the inside of your foot.

2 Then use the outside of your foot to push the ball forwards a little more. By alternating the inside, then outside of your foot, you will be able to dribble the ball in a straight line.

TOP TIP

When dribbling, the ball should be in front of you, but close enough to your feet so that another player cannot steal possession from you!

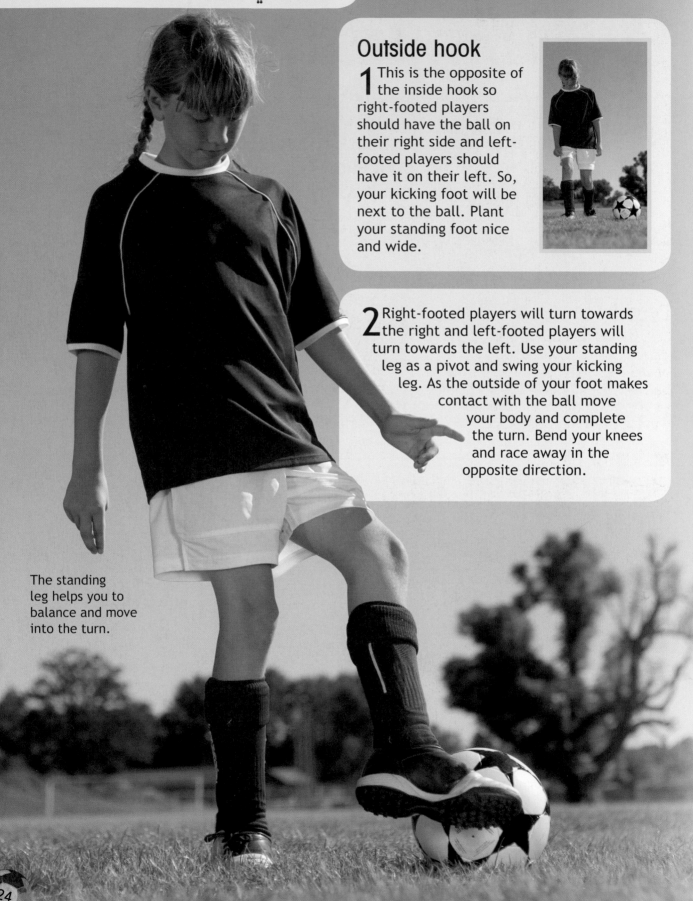

Outside hook

1 This is the opposite of the inside hook so right-footed players should have the ball on their right side and left-footed players should have it on their left. So, your kicking foot will be next to the ball. Plant your standing foot nice and wide.

2 Right-footed players will turn towards the right and left-footed players will turn towards the left. Use your standing leg as a pivot and swing your kicking leg. As the outside of your foot makes contact with the ball move your body and complete the turn. Bend your knees and race away in the opposite direction.

The standing leg helps you to balance and move into the turn.

Turning

In tight situations a player will often have to change direction to avoid an opponent and create space. Turning requires skill, control and balance so you need lots of practice. There are five basic turns shown here and over the page.

Drag back

This turn is for getting past defenders. Put your foot on top of the ball. Keep your eyes on the ball and drag it behind you. Then race away in the other direction, leaving the defender behind!

Inside hook

1 If you are right-footed, the ball should be on your left side and, if you are left-footed, the ball should be on your right side. Plant your standing foot close to the ball.

2 Using your standing leg as a pivot, swing your kicking foot around. (Right-footed players will turn from right to left and left-footed players will turn from left to right.)

3 As your body begins to move around, make contact with the ball using the inside of your foot and complete the turn. In a match situation this will happen fast!

Expert Turns

When you have mastered the drag back and the inside and outside hooks, it is time to move on to the two most difficult turns!

TOP TIP

Do not over-use these turns in a match, otherwise the opposition will be expecting them!

Stop turn

1 This turn is a great way of changing direction fast. As you are running with the ball, suddenly place your foot on top, to stop it dead.

2 Your marker will be surprised and will continue to run past you. While you have the advantage, carefully step over the ball.

3 After you have stepped over the ball, turn and take the ball in the opposite direction. Don't try and turn too fast or you will fall over!

The Cruyff turn

STAR PRO

As captain of Holland in the 1974 World Cup, **Johan Cruyff** was a master of the art of turning with speed and agility. His signature turn is still used today.

1 The key to this turn is convincing the opposition that you are about to pass the ball. Point to where you are pretending to pass.

2 Keeping up the act, plant your standing foot close to the ball. Pretend that you are going to use the other foot to pass.

Keep your eyes on the ball.

Use your arms for balance.

3 At the last moment, use your kicking foot to flick the ball behind you. The opposition player will not be expecting this!

STAR PRO

Portugal's **Cristiano Ronaldo** uses his pace and delicate skills to change direction, confuse the defender and create space for himself or a team mate.

4 Turn quickly. You should lose your marker. You are now in more space and can pass, shoot or dribble towards the goal.

27

Tackling

When the opposing team has the ball, you will need to win back possession. The most direct way of doing this is to make a tackle. You can either tackle a player from the front or the side. Tackles from behind are against the rules because they dangerous and could cause serious injuries.

Block tackle

This is the most common type of tackle and it can be appproached from the front or side. It can also be used for a 50-50 situation, which is when you and your opponent have an equal chance of winning the ball.

Safe tackling

Every player should learn how to tackle, not only defenders. When making a tackle, keep your eyes on the ball. The key thing is timing — a mis-timed tackle could cause injury to yourself or your opponent.

1 Get in close to your opponent and put her under pressure. Timing is important so wait until she is about to pass the ball or try to knock it past you before making the tackle.

2 Move forwards and use the inside of your foot to make the tackle. Try to keep your eyes on the ball. If the ball becomes stuck between your feet, get your foot underneath and lift the ball away.

TOP TIPS

• Be committed — a clumsy or half-hearted tackle can cause injury and result in a booking.

• Close down your opponent's space — you just might force them into making an error without even needing to make a tackle!

Sliding tackle

This type of tackle aims to clear the ball away from your opponent rather than winning possession. Like the block, it can be from the front or the side but NEVER from behind. Time your tackle so that you slide in just as your opponent is about to pass or shoot. As you run towards your opponent, bend your non-kicking leg and then use your laces to push the ball away.

Use your arm and elbow to cushion your fall.

Take care not to make contact with your opponent as this may injure them or give away a free kick.

Slide in low and try to get your leg around the ball to hook it away.

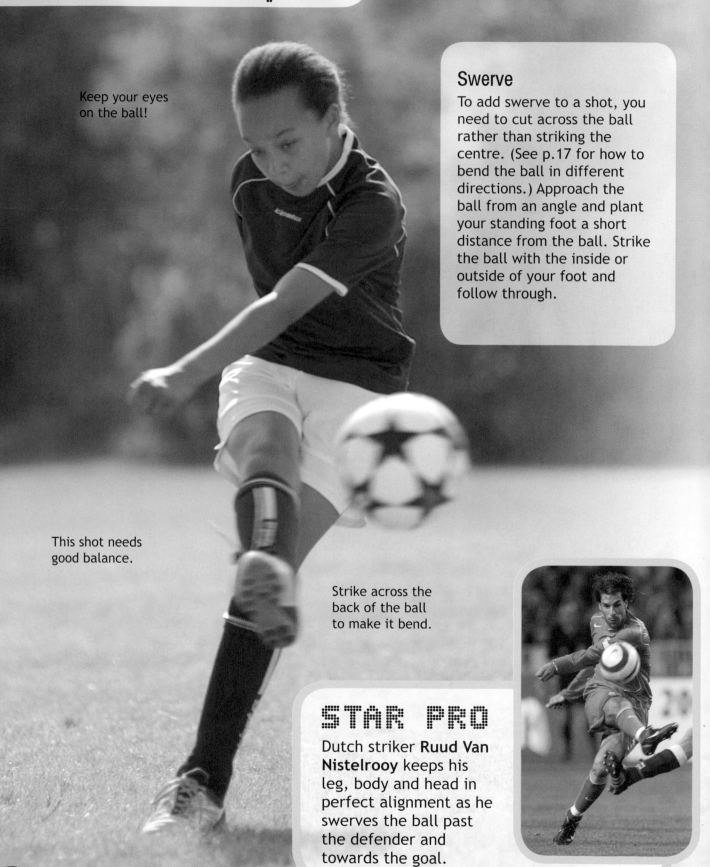

Keep your eyes on the ball!

Swerve

To add swerve to a shot, you need to cut across the ball rather than striking the centre. (See p.17 for how to bend the ball in different directions.) Approach the ball from an angle and plant your standing foot a short distance from the ball. Strike the ball with the inside or outside of your foot and follow through.

This shot needs good balance.

Strike across the back of the ball to make it bend.

STAR PRO

Dutch striker **Ruud Van Nistelrooy** keeps his leg, body and head in perfect alignment as he swerves the ball past the defender and towards the goal.

Shooting

Goals are what football is all about! To score a goal, a player can strike the ball in a number of ways and the technique is very similar to those used for passing (see p.14—15) and kicking (see p.16—17). Different parts of your foot alter the angle and power of the shot.

Shooting pratice

Line up some balls and take it in turns to try different types of shot. Every player should learn how to strike the ball, even defenders. In a match situation anything could happen, so wherever you play, you need to be able to shoot if a goalscoring opportunity comes your way!

TOP TIPS

• Keep your head still when striking the ball.

• To stop the ball rising too much, keep your body weight over the ball, not behind it.

Side foot

The simplest way to shoot is with the inside or outside of your foot. This type of shot is best for close range, when accuracy is more important than power. It is a great way of scoring when you have created space and only have the goalkeeper to beat.

Laces

The basics are the same as the driven pass (see p.15) but the shot is quicker and more powerful. Use your non-striking foot for balance and swing your striking leg back. Strike the ball hard and fast with your laces and follow through powerfully.

Chip

If you see the goalkeeper too far off the goal line, you can try a chip shot. (See p.14.) Point your foot down and aim for the underside of the ball. Lean backwards, strike the ball with a sharp, stabbing action and do not follow through.

Sharp Shooting

It's fantastic when your team wins and even better if you score a goal! Here are some of the most crowd-pleasing ways of scoring goals but be warned — even some of the world's top players find them difficult. Just relax, have fun and see what you can do.

Overhead kick

1 This shot works when you have your back to goal. Get in line with the ball and jump, using your non-kicking leg to propel you upwards. As you start to fall backwards, quickly bring your kicking foot up.

2 Strike the back of the ball when your upper body is almost horizontal to the ground. Your non-kicking foot should be on the ground. This scissor action with your legs gives the shot power.

3 As you fall, stretch out your hand to soften the impact. Try to fall sideways and use your arms to cushion your fall. It is best to practise this technique on soft ground to prevent injury!

Which shot?

The type of shot you use depends on how the ball is coming towards you, the angle between you and the goal, and the position of the defenders. In a match, you might only have a split-second to decide which shot to use, so quick thinking and good technique are vital.

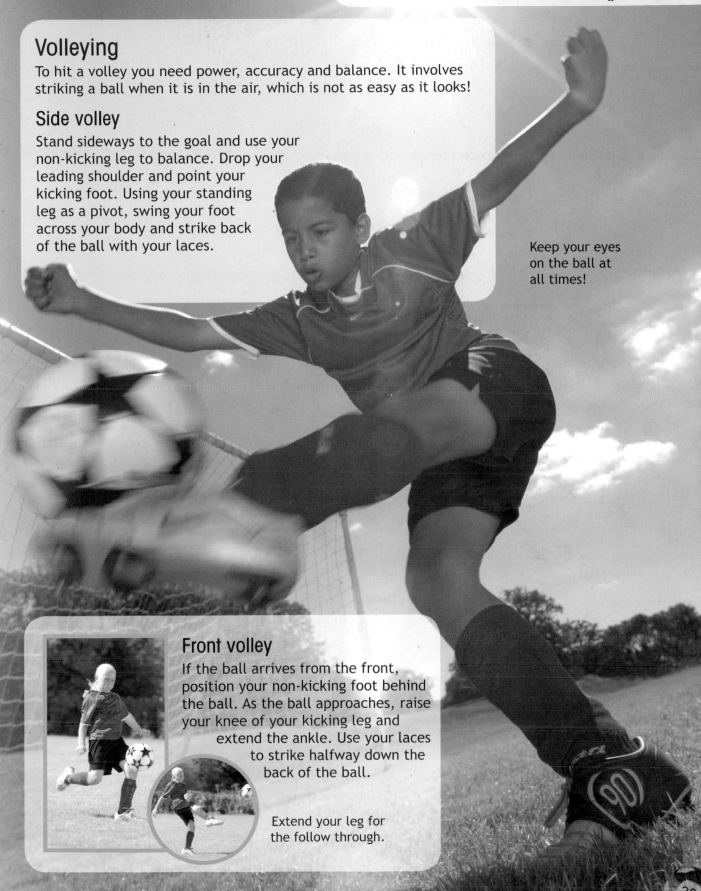

Volleying

To hit a volley you need power, accuracy and balance. It involves striking a ball when it is in the air, which is not as easy as it looks!

Side volley

Stand sideways to the goal and use your non-kicking leg to balance. Drop your leading shoulder and point your kicking foot. Using your standing leg as a pivot, swing your foot across your body and strike back of the ball with your laces.

Keep your eyes on the ball at all times!

Front volley

If the ball arrives from the front, position your non-kicking foot behind the ball. As the ball approaches, raise your knee of your kicking leg and extend the ankle. Use your laces to strike halfway down the back of the ball.

Extend your leg for the follow through.

33

2 Bend your front knee and get down low to the ground. Bring your arm forwards and release the ball when it is level with your front foot. Rolling is a great way of turning defence into attack!

Rolling the ball

1 This underarm technique is only suitable for short distances because it doesn't generate much power. Hold the ball in the palm of your strongest hand and step forwards with your opposite leg.

The leg opposite to your throwing arm should be forwards.

Overarm throw

1 An overarm throw is a good way of starting a quick counter-attack. Stand sideways on and put the palm of your throwing hand behind the ball. Use your non-throwing arm to point at the target.

2 Place your opposite leg forward and bring your throwing arm over your shoulder. Release the ball at head height. Follow through until your throwing arm is extended.

TOP TIP

Goalkeepers need to be loud! Your team mates need to know that you have the ball covered.

Goalkeeping

Goalkeepers are more than just the last line of defence. A good goalkeeper is the backbone of the team. As well as saving goals, he can launch attacking moves. A goalkeeper should be strong, athletic and able to read the game.

STAR PRO

England goalkeeper **Paul Robinson** makes use of the strength and power in his arms, legs and body to distribute the ball quickly and accurately to a team mate.

Goal kick

1 With both hands, hold the ball out in front of you at about waist height. Keep your eyes on the ball. Take a few quick steps and release the ball.

2 Swing your kicking leg back and strike the bottom half of the ball with your laces. Follow through with your kicking leg for maximum power.

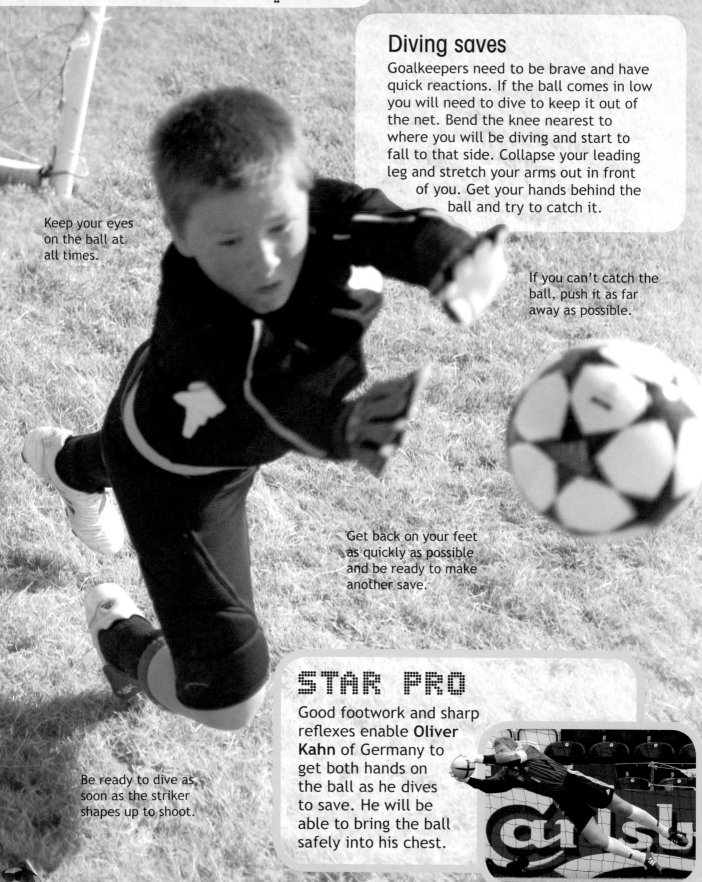

Diving saves

Goalkeepers need to be brave and have quick reactions. If the ball comes in low you will need to dive to keep it out of the net. Bend the knee nearest to where you will be diving and start to fall to that side. Collapse your leading leg and stretch your arms out in front of you. Get your hands behind the ball and try to catch it.

Keep your eyes on the ball at all times.

If you can't catch the ball, push it as far away as possible.

Get back on your feet as quickly as possible and be ready to make another save.

Be ready to dive as soon as the striker shapes up to shoot.

STAR PRO

Good footwork and sharp reflexes enable **Oliver Kahn** of Germany to get both hands on the ball as he dives to save. He will be able to bring the ball safely into his chest.

Hands-On Saves

In some ways, learning how to be a goalkeeper is more difficult than learning to be an outfield player. After all goalkeepers need strong hands as well as skilful feet. A goalkeeper also needs to be calm under pressure and able to choose the best technique for the situation he is in.

Clench each hand into a fist with your thumbs on top.

Catching balls at chest height and above

1 Stretch your arms and get your hands behind the ball. Spread your fingers wide with your thumbs close together to form a 'w' shape.

2 As the ball comes towards you hold the 'w' shape and keep your hands relaxed. Catch the ball and then clutch it safely to your chest.

Punching

If you are unable to catch a cross, you will need to punch the ball away. Put your clenched hands together and keep your wrists strong. Aim for the bottom half of the ball and punch it hard to get maximum height and distance in your clearance.

TOP TIP

Be alert and keep your eyes on the game at all times. When are about to make a save, keep your head still and your body weight forwards.

Cup and scoop

If a ball comes towards you between chest and knee height bend your knees, turn your palms upwards and **cup** the ball towards your body.

If the ball comes towards you at a lower height bend down low, stretch out your arms with the palms up and gather or **scoop** the ball.

Practice Drills

When you have learnt the basic techniques it is important that you keep on practising them. Here are some group drills to try in your next training session. They are a fun way of testing how well you remember what you have learnt and they also help you to get used to playing under pressure!

Attack and defence drill

This drill requires speed, control and awareness. Each player has a ball and the object is to kick the other players' balls away while keeping possession of your own ball. You will need to use your tackling technique to rob the other players of possession but at the same time you must dribble and turn to avoid losing your ball. This drill will not only test your dribbling, tackling and turning but it will also help you to start thinking tactically.

Tag football

This is a traditional game of tag, with a football twist. Each player has a ball at their feet and a bib tucked into the back of their shorts. The object is to grab as many bibs as you can without losing your own. You must also keep your ball under control!

This drill is all about balance, control and awareness. You also need to time your grab just right!

Star drill

This drill can be used to practise just about any technique! Arrange some cones in a circle (one for each player) and place a cone in the centre. Each player stands by a cone with a ball at their feet. The coach gives each technique a number. When he shouts a number the players move towards the centre cone while performing the technique.

When the coach shouts "four!" the players have to dribble to the centre, do an inside hook turn and then dribble back. This drill also tests players' mental agility!

Shark attack!

Each player has a ball, except one. He is the 'shark' and must try to steal the balls from all the other players. For most players this drill is about keeping possession but the 'shark' is on the attack and must use well-timed tackles to win the ball. Players should take turns at being the 'shark'.

Basic Laws

The game of football has seventeen laws which are constantly being revised and updated. Football laws are mostly just common sense and are about playing fairly, safely and respectfully. Here are some important laws to remember.

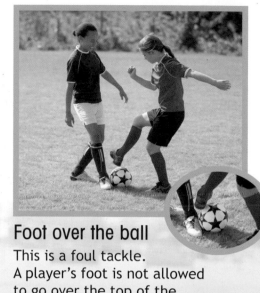

Foot over the ball

This is a foul tackle. A player's foot is not allowed to go over the top of the ball as this could cause injury to an opponent.

Offside is judged from the moment the ball is played, not from when it is received.

TOP TIPS

• A player is only offside if he or she is involved in active play.

• The ball must be played forwards for a player to be offside — sideways or backwards are allowed.

• You cannot be offside in your own half or if an opponent plays the ball to you.

Tackle from behind

This is also a foul tackle. Tackles from behind are dangerous and often result in injury to the player and a red card for the tackler.

Handball

Only the goalkeeper is allowed to touch the ball with his hands in open play. If a defender does this in his penalty area he is likely to be shown a red card.

OFFICIALS

The referee is the person in charge of the match. He ensures that the game is played according to the laws of football. He is supported by two assistants, one on each touchline.

Fouls and infringements usually result in a free kick for the opposition. For persistent breaches of the laws, the referee shows a yellow card. If a player receives two yellow cards in a match he will be sent off the pitch. Serious fouls result in a red card and a player must leave the pitch immediately.

The offside rule

This rule is designed to prevent attackers from goal-hanging. The rule is that a player must not be in front of the last defender when the ball is played to them.

Onside

Staying onside is about timing. The red attacker is in line with the blue defenders. He must not move past them until his team mate has played the ball.

Offside

The red attacker has moved too early! He is now beyond the last defender and therefore will be offside when the ball is played.

Attacking Skills

Learning the correct techniques is only part of what you need to be a good footballer — you also need to learn how to perform well in a match situation. This means being able to work as part of a team and also being able to use your techniques under pressure. Here are some attacking match skills.

STAR PRO

Strength, determination, concentration and great technique drive **Wayne Rooney** past two defenders and towards the goal for England.

The take over

These players are practising a pass called a take over. It is a way of changing direction quickly. As one player dribbles, her team mate runs towards her. As he gets closer, she pushes the ball forwards a little way. The other player takes the ball and dribbles away in the other direction.

One-two or wall pass

1 This is a simple but effective way to get through the defence. It requires teamwork and good communication (both verbal and non verbal). Instead of trying to dribble past your opponent, send a short pass to the feet of a team mate.

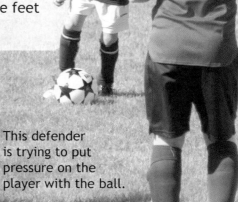

The defenders are holding the line, hoping to catch the blue attacker offside.

This defender is trying to put pressure on the player with the ball.

Losing your marker

1 It can be hard to win possession if you are being closely marked so here is a way of losing your marker. As your team mate shapes to pass the ball, pretend to move.

2 As the defender follows you, quickly change direction. If you do this quickly enough, your marker will be fooled and you will be free to receive the pass.

TOP TIP

To get past defenders, adopt a sprinting stance — keep your body position low and bend your knees. Then you will be able to turn on a sudden burst of speed and leave the defenders trailing in your wake!

2 Continue to run forwards, past the defenders. Shout to your team mate to make her aware of your run.

This attacker knows that she must stay onside if the move is going to work.

3 Your team mate should quickly pass the ball directly into your path, giving you the opportunity to race away.

The dummy

The angle of your body is very important.

1 This is a simple way of fooling your opponent. As the defender approaches, angle your body as if you are going to pass the ball with the inside of your foot.

2 The defender will move in the direction you are pretending to go in. When she is fully committed, move your foot around the ball and use the outside of your foot to take the ball away in the opposite direction!

3 You are now free to dribble the ball away. By the time the defender realises she has gone the wrong way you will be long gone.

The defender is fooled!

One v One Attack

Attackers need to be confident on the ball and willing to take on defenders. With skill and clever play, you can create a goalscoring opportunity for yourself or a team mate out of nothing. Here are a few skilful ways of getting past your opponent.

The nutmeg

1 Only confident players should attempt this cheeky skill. As the defender comes towards you, knock the ball through his legs.

2 Run past the defender and collect the ball. This only works if a defender is not concentrating so don't try it too often!

STAR PRO

The strength and pace of the Ivory Coast's **Didier Drogba** ensures that his full body shields the ball from a despairing defender.

Step over

1 You need two skilful feet for this. As the defender approaches, pretend that you are about to pass the ball with the outside of one foot. Instead of passing, step all the way over the ball.

2 The defender will think you are going to pass and follow the direction of your foot. So you can simply use the outside of your other foot and race off in the opposite direction!

Defending Skills

Being a good defender is not just about making tackles. Defenders need to have good communication, awareness and technique. They must also try to break down attacks by reading the game and putting attackers under pressure.

TOP TIP

The key to defending is pressure. If you close down attackers' space and put them under pressure they are more likely to make a mistake and give the ball away.

Intercepting a pass

1 This is a simple way of winning the ball without making a tackle. The reds are on the attack. As the blues close down the space, the red attacker prepares to pass the ball.

2 As the red attacker passes, the blue defender reads the pass and quickly intercepts it. The blues have put pressure on the reds, read the game and won possession.

Zonal marking

This system of marking is not widely used but is an interesting alternative to man marking. The blues have divided the penalty area into zones. Each defender, including the goalkeeper marks their own zone instead of an individual player. In this system the defenders focus on the ball rather than the opposing attackers.

At set pieces the defenders stand goal side.

This defender must keep her eyes on the ball and the red attacker!

The attacker will try and lose his marker.

Man marking

This is the most common type of marking. Defenders are assigned to mark an individual attacker for the whole match. That means that the defender must be aware of what the attacker is doing at all times, even when he doesn't have the ball. Don't get caught out just watching the ball!

STAR PRO

French defensive midfielder **Claude Makelele** (left) uses all his experience to get ahead of an opposing forward and force him away from the penalty area danger zone.

Team Defending

Teamwork is a key part of effective defending. Apart from the goalkeeper, the defence is what stands in the way of the opposition scoring goals. Intelligent positioning and playing as a co-ordinated defensive unit are vital match skills to learn.

Defending a corner

The reds have a corner. If the blues get their positioning right, the reds have less chance of scoring. Each red attacker is being closely marked by a blue defender. The defenders stand between the attackers and the goal, watching the flight of the ball while also making sure the attackers don't make a sneaky move away from them. There are also two extra defenders guarding each goal post.

Offside trap

1 A well-organised defence can also work together to catch the attackers offside. The defence stands in a line as the attacker is about to pass the ball to her team mate. At this point, the red attacker without the ball is onside.

2 Just as the attacker is about to pass the ball, the blue defenders all take a step forwards in a line. Then, as the ball is played they raise their arms to show that the red attacker is offside. The blues have used teamwork to win a free kick.

Defending a free kick

When the attackers have a free kick within shooting distance, the best way to defend is to organise a wall. The goalkeeper positions a line of defenders so that it blocks the attackers' view of the near post. The goalkeeper then covers the far post, making it harder for the attacker to score.

The goalkeeper should have a clear sight of the ball.

Make sure that the wall stands firm!

STAR PROS

Germany organise a five-man wall to defend a free kick. Usually the goalkeeper and the player closest to the ball organise the position of the wall.

49

STAR PRO

Czech goalkeeper **Petr Cech** goes full length to make a save. His hands, arms and body are behind the line of the ball.

Aim for height and distance.

Goalkeepers have to be brave under pressure!

High balls

If the ball is in the air, it is difficult to catch it cleanly, especially if an attacker is putting you under pressure. Goalkeepers need to be brave and confident in these situations. Just keep your eyes on the ball and try to punch the ball away as high and as far as possible.

Goalkeeper in Action

In a match, goalkeepers need to be able to react under pressure. Often the goalkeeper is the only player standing between the opposition and a sure-fire goal — if she makes a brilliant save she will be a hero but if she makes a mistake it could prove very costly for the team.

TOP TIP

Penalties favour the attacker — if they strike the ball into the corners, they will probably score. So, when you are practising penalties, forget about the corners! Mark out a smaller goal with cones and practise making saves in this area.

Penalties

1 Every goalkeeper has a different idea about the best way to save a penalty, but here are the basics. Before the attacker strikes the ball, focus your mind on what you are about to do. You should try to ignore any crowd noise.

2 Goalkeepers usually decide which way they are going to dive before the ball has been struck. If you guess right, you stand a good chance of saving the penalty. But remember, a well struck penalty is almost impossible to save!

Narrowing the angle

1 If you are faced with a one versus one situation with a striker, you need to make it harder for them to score.

2 Come out of the goal and move forwards in line with the ball. This gives the striker less space to shoot and blocks his view of the goal.

The Dead Ball

When the ball has gone out of play or the referee has stopped for a foul or infringement, it is known as a dead ball. You should practise these situations with your team mates so that you can make the most of these opportunities in a match.

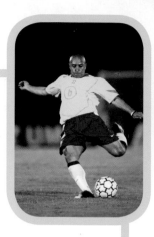

Throw in

1 Throw ins are awarded when the opposition kick the ball over the touchline. To start, position your feet on or behind the touchline.

2 Hold the ball behind your head, with both hands. Bring it forwards quickly and release it before it is level with your head.

Free kick

When the referee awards a free kick, he will tell you where it should be taken and when to take it. If it is a direct free kick within scoring distance, the opposition will set up a wall (see p.49). In that situation you need to bend the ball (see p.17) round the wall or chip it (see p.14, p.32) over the top of the wall.

Penalty

A penalty is great chance to score but it is also a high-pressure situation. Try to stay calm and choose your spot before you strike the ball.

The whole of the ball must be inside the area known as the corner arc.

Taking a corner

A corner kick is awarded if the opposition knock the ball over their own goal line. The corner must be taken from the corner arc on the same side of the pitch that the ball crossed the goal line. A corner is often a great opportunity to score a headed goal so it is good idea for the tallest players to come forwards.

The opposition must be at least 9.1 metres (10 yards) away.

Short corner

You could try a short corner for variation. Instead of playing a long ball to the near or far post, make a short pass to your team mate. He can either cross the ball in or pass it back to you so that you can make a run into the penalty area.

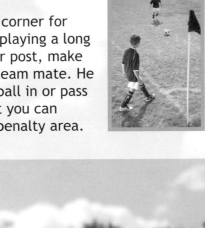

Try to aim the ball at the near or far posts as they are difficult areas to defend.

It is possible to score directly from a corner!

Tricks of the Trade

Professional footballers have such great technique that they are often able to dazzle the crowds (and surprise the opposition!) with amazing displays of skill. Have a go at some of these tricks and you will be a superstar show off in no time!

Cheeky flick

Put the ball between your feet. Jump and flick the ball up behind you. Then turn and volley the ball. You should practise this move in training before you try it in a match.

STAR PRO

Brazil's World Cup inspiration **Ronaldo** demonstrates balance and clever footwork as he conjures up a cheeky trick to unbalance two Argentine defenders. A trick like this requires great technique and a lot of confidence!

Balance

This trick is for showing off purposes only. Try balancing the ball on your head or shoulders — it is much harder than it looks!

STAR PRO

Sweden's **Freddie Ljungberg** could do with a safety net as he launches himself into a spectacular overhead effort. He makes this difficult shot look effortless. See p.32 for a step-by-step guide to overhead kicks.

Keepy uppies require a lot of ball control in this position because you can only move your feet!

Keepy uppies

They look impressive and are a great way of practising ball control (see p.18-19). Use your feet and thighs to prevent the ball from touching the ground. Try to stay relaxed.

TOP TIPS

Only attempt a trick in a match if you feel confident and be prepared to look a little foolish if it doesn't work out!

The Match

Playing in a match is a great way to test how much you have learnt! You must try to remember everything that the coach has taught you so that you play as part of the team.

The goalkeeper should always be ready for action!

Turning on the skill

As the red player prepares to make a tackle, the white player uses the techniques she has learnt to go past him. With a great piece of skill, she executes an inside hook turn (see p.25).

Awareness

Who wants the ball? The red team has a free kick but there is no one to pass to!

Corner

The reds are defending the goal well but the whites need to bring more players forwards.

Goal?

The attacker has only the goalkeeper to beat. His body position is excellent as he shapes up to shoot. He is going to strike the ball with his laces (see p.31) and if he swerves the shot to the left, the goalkeeper will surely be beaten.

Skills in action

The red player has noticed her team mate on the edge of the penalty area. She tries to aim her driven pass (see p.15) right into his path. This is a great example of vision.

Close control

The white player has controlled the ball very well (see p.18-19). Her team mate is telling her that he wants to receive the pass but the white player may choose to go on herself.

50-50

This ball could go either way as both players try their hardest to get to it first. Both players are determined!

STAR PRO

Ronaldinho of Brazil has been described by the Dutch coach Frank Rijkaard as "the player who has absolutely everything." In 2005 he won the FIFA World Player of the Year and European Footballer of the Year.

Keep practising

Even the best footballers in the world have to practise. Technique can always be improved and new skills learnt. Remember to keep training both feet and your weaker foot will gradually become stronger.

The Future

Now that you have learnt how to play football like a star professional, the next step is to join a team and keep playing the game. Your technique will continue to improve with regular coaching sessions and by playing in competitive matches. It is also a great way to keep your body fit and active.

The FIFA World Cup

Every player dreams of playing in the World Cup Finals. The competition has taken place every four years since 1930 and is a chance for the best teams to shine in front of the whole world. It is an inspirational occasion for everyone.

STAR TEAM

Greece triumphed against the odds at the European Championships in Portugal in 2004 thanks to tactical discipline, high fitness levels and outstanding team spirit.

Have fun!

The best thing about football is that it can be played by people of any age, ability, race, sex or background. So you have no excuse not to get out there and start playing!

Glossary

A

Astro boots — football boots with small pimples on the sole, suitable for playing on artificial or firm surfaces.

C

Centre spot — the point in the centre of the pitch where the match starts and re-starts after a goal.

Chip — a pass or shot in which the bottom of the ball is struck with a short stabbing motion with no follow through.

Corner arc — the area at the corner of the pitch where the corner kick is taken.

Corner flag - a flag marking the corner arc.

Corner kick — an attacking dead ball situation arising when the defending team puts the ball over their own goal line.

Cross — to kick or pass the ball across the pitch, usually into the penalty area to create a goalscoring opportunity.

Cruyff turn — a deceptive turn named after the world-famous Dutch footballer of the 1970s, Johan Cruyff.

Cup — the technique a goalkeeper uses to catch a ball between chest and knee height.

D

Dead ball — a break in play, often due to a free kick or throw in.

Drag back — when a player drags the ball behind him and executes a quick turn and change of direction.

Dribble — moving the ball with lots of small, quick kicks, usually with both feet.

Driven pass — a powerful pass struck with the laces which can travel over a long distance.

Dummy — to pretend to pass or shoot in one direction to deceive an opponent and then to move the opposite way.

E

Eighteen yard box — the larger marked area around the goal, in which a penalty may be given.

F

Far post — the goal post furthest away from the point of attack, e.g. a corner or free kick.

FIFA — the world of football's governing body, the Fédération Internationale de Football Association.

Foul — an infringement of the laws of football, such as when a player trips, kicks or pushes an opponent (accidentally or deliberately).

Free kick — when play is stopped by the referee and a kick awarded to the opposing side, usually due to a foul or infringement.

G

Goal — 1. The nets supported by two posts and a crossbar at each end of the pitch, where the goalkeepers stand.
2. When the ball crosses the line into the goal area and a team scores.

Goal line — the line linking the corner flags with the goal posts.

H

Halfway line — the marked-out line that separates one half of the pitch from the other.

Handball — a type of foul. It is illegal for an outfield player to touch the ball with his or her hand in open play.

I

Infringement — to break one of the laws of football.

Instep — the upper surface of the foot or boot, also called the laces.

Intercept — to steal possession of or get in the way of an opponent's pass.

L

Laces — the upper surface of the foot or boot, also called the instep.

Long lofted kick — a powerful kick using the laces that rises above the ground.

M

Mark — to position yourself close to an opponent so that it is difficult for him or her to receive or pass the ball.

Match — a competitive game, usually comprising two halves of 45 minutes.
Mini pitch — a small pitch especially for young players.

N

Near post — the goal post nearest to the point of attack, such as a corner or free kick.
Nutmeg — to kick the ball through an opponent's legs and then collect it on the other side.

O

Offside — when an attacker has moved beyond the last defender as the ball is played forwards.
One-two — a quick back-and-forth pass between two players, also known as a wall pass.

P

Penalty — a specific kind of free kick awarded when an attacker is fouled in the penalty area.
Penalty spot — the place from where the penalty is taken.
Pitch — the field of play.
Possession — to have the ball.
Punch — when the goalkeeper uses his or her fists to make a save.
Push pass — a short pass with the side of the foot, also known as a side foot pass.

R

Reading the game — playing the game intelligently e.g. using tactical knowledge to improve positioning, passing, tackling and intercepting.
Red card — a player is shown this after a particularly bad offence or after receiving two yellow cards in a match.
Referee — the official in charge of the match, who checks that the laws of football are not broken.
Referee's assistants — the flag-carrying officials positioned on either touchline who help the referee.

S

Scoop — the technique a goalkeeper uses to catch a ball below knee height.
Score — to get a goal.
Sent off — when a player receives a red card and is sent from the field of play.
Shin pads — protective shields for the shins and ankles, usually worn underneath the socks.
Shoot — to aim a kick or pass at the goal.
Side foot pass — a short pass with the side of the foot, also known as a push pass.
Six yard box — the small marked-out area around the goal.
Stop turn — a way of changing direction quickly by stopping the ball at speed.
Studs — the grips on the sole of a football boot.
Swerve — to kick or strike across the back of the ball so that it bends in the opposite direction.

T

Tackle — to fairly challenge a player for the ball. A tackle can be block or sliding.
Throw in — a throw from the touchline awarded by the referee when the opposition have kicked the ball out of play.
Touchlines — the two lines running down the length of the pitch.

V

Volley — to kick the ball before it touches the ground, usually as a shot on goal.

W

Wall — a line of two or more players defending their goal against a free kick.
Wall pass — a quick back-and-forth pass between two players, also known as a one-two.
Wedge — to trap the ball under your foot to control it.

Y

Yellow card — this is shown by the referee for a serious offence of persistent offending.

Index

DK

LONDON, NEW YORK, MUNICH,
MELBOURNE AND DELHI

Senior Art Editor	Guy Harvey
Senior Editor	Catherine Saunders
Publishing Manager	Simon Beecroft
Brand Manager	Lisa Lanzarini
Category Publisher	Alex Allan
DTP Designers	Lauren Egan and Hanna Ländin
Production Controller	Amy Bennett
Coach and Technical Adviser	Mark Drabwell
Star Pro Panels	Keir Radnedge
Picture Researcher	Will Jones

First published in Great Britain in 2006 by
Dorling Kindersley Limited
80 Strand, London WC2R ORL
06 07 08 09 10 10 9 8 7 6 5 4 3 2 1
Copyright © 2006 Dorling Kindersley Limited

ISBN-13 978-1-40531-123-6
ISBN-10 1-4053-1123-1

Colour reproduction by MDP Ltd., UK
Printed and bound in Italy by L.E.G.O.

Discover more at
www.dk.com

The Publisher would like
to thank the following
libraries for permission to
reproduce their images:
(b= bottom, c-centre, l=left, r=right,
t=top)
Adrian DENNIS/AFP/Getty Images:
25tr. Alex Livesey/Getty Images: 59bl.
Alexander Hassenstein/Bongarts/Getty
Images: 49br. ANTONIO SIMOES/AFP/Getty
Images: 27tr. Ben Radford/Getty Images:
59tl. Christof Koepsel/Bongarts/Getty
Images: 30br. FRANCOIS XAVIER MARIT/AFP/
Getty Images: 36br; 50tl. FRANCK FIFE/
AFP/Getty Images: 47br. Jamie McDonald/
Allsport: 14br. JAVIER SORIANO/AFP/Getty
Images: 19br. © Karoly Arvai/Reuters/
Corbis: 55tr. KIM JAE-HWAN/AFP/Getty
Images: 28tl. Lars Baron/Bongarts/Getty
Images: 32br. Laurence Griffiths/Getty
Images: 21bl. Mary Evans Picture Library:
6cbl. Matthew Peters/Manchester United
via Getty Images: 42c. Mike Hewitt/Getty
Images: 45bl. MIGUEL ROJO/AFP/Getty
Images: 13cl. Shaun Botterill/Getty Images:
23c; 35cr; 52tr. © SPORTSPHOTO AGENCY/
CORBIS SYGMA: 10c. © Stockdisc Classic/
Alamy: 9br. Stuart Franklin/Bongarts/Getty
Images: 58tr. © Toby Melville/Reuters/
Corbis: 17br. VANDERLEI ALMEIDA/AFP/
Getty Images: 54bl.Vladimir Rys/Bongarts/
Getty Images: 41tr. Will Jones: 9tr.

DORLING KINDERSLEY would like to thank the following young
footballers for making the photoshoot such great fun: Biyi Adetunji,
Todd Armstrong, Brooke Barfoot, Daniel Barnes, Bianca Bragg,
Louis Claridge, Niall Crouch, Tricia Gould, Morgan Hammond,
Jake Holmes, Sian Horrigan, Ashleigh James, Abigail Kemball Cook,
Ellie King, Niall McDonough, Michael McManamon, Ria Melvin,
Piero Monastero, Sabrina Monastero, Trai Sackett,
Bethany Stanfield, Beth Wood and Charlie Young.